MW01656879

Say to My Soul Rise Up

"A Journey of Self-Discovery, Freedom, & Fulfillment"

JOCELYN JONES

Dedication

First, to my husband, thank you for choosing me. Thank you for walking with me, carrying me, and supporting me throughout this process. Thank you for being my safe space, where I could remove the mask, let down the "draw bridge" to my fortress, and be completely vulnerable. Thank you for not only seeing me but also hearing me, acknowledging me, and understanding me. Thank you for being patient with me and loving me through this evolution.

To Kevin and Tre, you both have been with me and "seen" me throughout this journey. I thank you for being patient with me as I walked through this and for being gentle with me as I allowed you both to express how my trauma impacted your lives. Thank you for graciously accepting my apologies. By the way, I'm still not one of your little friends…lol.

To Darius McClure, thank you for creating and offering a space for me to heal. A space where my vulnerability was my strength and not my weakness. In a time when I was open, ready, and willing to do the work. The lessons learned, the space given, along with all of the laughter and tears made it easy to continue doing the heart work daily. Your coaching, mentorship, guidance, prayer, and covering have kept me focused on the importance of this journey. I am forever grateful for your obedience, and I am honored to be able to continue to glean from your faith, your wisdom, and your guidance.

Last but definitely not least, I echo the words of David in Psalm 124:1-6, "If it had not been the Lord who was on our (my) side," Let Israel now say, "If it had not been the Lord who was on our (my) side When men rose up against us (me), Then they would have [quickly] swallowed us (me) alive, When their wrath was kindled against us (me); Then the waters would have engulfed us (me), The torrent would have swept over our (my) soul; Then the raging waters would have swept over our (my) soul." Blessed be the Lord, Who has not given us (me) as prey to be torn by their teeth. God, you've been a good, good father and I thank you for keeping and protecting me.

Table of Contents

Foreword

I met Jocelyn in the summer of 1995. I was expecting my first child; she was already a mom. We were both so young, but we immediately became friends. Then we grew into sisters. We were both Believers, but we had so much growing to do in learning and yielding to His will for our lives.

Over the years, we have grown closer and closer, as our individual walks with God have grown more and more comprehensive. We have been used by the Holy Spirit in each other's lives, and we have been able to share our joys, our pain, and the lessons we have learned: some we learned the easy way, and others we had to learn the hard way! But God!

This guided journal has been lovingly and thoughtfully created for each of you…with the hope and prayer that it will help you to hear the voice of God and to meet Him wherever you are in your walk with Him. This journal invites you to jump into God's will for your life, as you learn to hear His voice, confront your fear, and as you ask God to reveal His will for your life. There are guides to help you pray more specifically for guidance, clarity, and revelation every step of the way.

I pray that you embrace this guided journal as your opportunity to initiate, develop, or deepen your relationship with God. Read the Scriptures, speak the prayers, and take notes as you grow closer to Him.

Know that Jocelyn has experienced her own deep walk with the Master and has grown from a young Believer to a minister of the Gospel. This journal is her personal invitation to you to meet God on His terms and to use this guidance as a foundation to further develop your relationship with Him. Take advantage of the guided opportunities to chart your spiritual growth and write out your affirmations, as you experience His gift of spiritual growth…designed by the Father, just for you!

Read, write, pray, and discover!

DeeDee Washington, Ph.D.

"For I know the plans I have for you," declares the Lord, "plans to prosper you and not to harm you, plans to give you hope and a future".

Jeremiah 29:11

Introduction

Welcome to My Guided Journal!

This journal is designed to help you explore your thoughts, set meaningful goals, and reflect on your experiences. It is a self-paced guided journal, allowing you to take as much time as you need to work through each session. My hope is that by the time you complete this book, you will find your soul elevated to a level of freedom, joy, and peace that is indescribable to those who haven't experienced it themselves. I encourage you to share your journey with others, inspiring them to embark on their own paths of self-discovery.

Use this journal as a sacred space to document your journey. Reflect regularly, be honest with yourself, and celebrate your progress, no matter how small. Your spiritual path is unique and personal, and this journal is a tool to help you stay connected and intentional.

The book is divided into three sessions, each containing seven thought-provoking and inspiring messages, along with mental and heart work exercises. Use this book to write openly and honestly and enjoy the process of self-discovery.

Affirmations often articulated as "I Am" statements, are simple yet powerful statements that you can repeat to influence thought patterns and behaviors. The most common form of affirmation is the "I Am" statement, where you declare positive qualities or achievements about yourself. For example, one might say, "I am confident," "I am capable of achieving my goals," or "I am worthy of love." Incorporate these positive declarations to challenge and overcome negative thoughts.

Use mindfulness techniques to navigate through the challenging parts. Mindfulness is about being aware and present in the moment. It means paying attention to your thoughts, feelings, and the world around you without judging or reacting to them. Practicing mindfulness can help reduce anxiety, improve how you handle emotions, increase focus, and boost overall mental well-being.

Jocelyn Jones

A Prayer of Release

Dear God,

I ask that you gently remove anything that is preventing me from loving myself fully and unconditionally. Remove that which is preventing me from believing in myself wholeheartedly and consistently and that which is keeping me from my joy, peace blessings, and success. Remove those barriers that I have placed around myself and my blessings in moments of fear, and the blocks that I have created when I push down my pain to appease others or "keep" the peace. Help me and allow me to know and accept my worth, calling, and anointing. Release anything that's not built upon love, and Your will for my life. I humbly ask that it all be done through peace, love, and grace.

In Jesus' name, I pray,

Amen

SESSION 1

Take the Leap

Preparing to "take the leap" mentally and spiritually involves fostering a mindset of resilience, courage, and clarity, as well as connecting with your deeper sense of purpose and inner strength.

As you work through the pages of this section:

Identify Your Why: Reflect on why you want to take this leap. Understanding your motivations can provide clarity and drive.

Assess Readiness: Evaluate your current mental, emotional, and spiritual state to determine if you are ready to start on this journey.

Build Confidence: Practice affirmations and positive self-talk to build confidence and reduce self-doubt.

Embrace Challenges: View challenges as opportunities for growth. Develop a mindset that sees setbacks as temporary and surmountable.

Stress Management: Practice stress management techniques such as deep breathing, mindfulness, or exercise to maintain mental well-being.

Seek Support: Surround yourself with a supportive community that encourages and motivates you.

By integrating these mental and spiritual preparation steps, you can build a strong foundation to take the leap with confidence, clarity, and a deep sense of purpose.

Calm Your Fears

"Fear not, for I am with you; be not dismayed, for I am your God; I will strengthen you, I will help you, I will uphold you with my righteous right hand."

Isaiah 41:10

This prayer is not a plea for the removal of all fear, but rather an invitation to face it with courage and grace. It acknowledges the presence of fear, embracing it as a part of the human experience, while simultaneously seeking strength and resilience to navigate its presence. It is a compass guiding us toward a calmer state of being. It is a reminder that we are not alone in our struggles and that there is a source of strength beyond ourselves waiting to be accessed.

Dear God,

I come before you, heavy with the weight of fear. It whispers in my ear, amplifying doubts and uncertainties. It paints vivid pictures of potential disasters, robbing me of peace and joy. Guide my mind to clarity, and my heart to courage. Help me to see the truth beyond the veil of fear, reminding me that You are always present, a constant source of strength and comfort. I release my anxieties into Your loving embrace. Help me to discern the roots of my fears, leading me to address them with wisdom and compassion. Grant me the serenity to accept the things I cannot change, the courage to change the things I can, and the wisdom to know the difference.

In the midst of my fear, I choose to trust in Your unwavering love and guidance. I believe in Your plan for my life, even when it seems shrouded in uncertainty. Fill me with peace that surpasses all understanding. Let Your love wash over me, calming my anxieties and replacing fear with faith.

In Jesus' name, I pray,

Amen

Heart Work

Intentional Breaths: Close your eyes, drop your shoulders, and release the tension. Now, take a deep breath and slowly exhale. Repeat 4 times. When you're done, come back to this page and write out your morning prayer.

Morning Prayer:

____

____

____

____

What is causing this fear? Is it fear of rejection? Do you feel unworthy? Is self-doubt taking up space in your mind? Sometimes it helps to write out what is causing the fear.

____

____

____

____

Mindful Intentions: Think about a fear, give it your full attention for just a moment. Imagine writing it on a whiteboard in big bold letters. Now see yourself erasing the fear from the whiteboard and as you do the fear is being removed from your conscience. Exhale as the fear disappears. Notice how your mind and body respond.

Positive Affirmations: Take this time to write out 1 or 2 positive affirmations that you can repeat to help calm your fear(s).

____

____

Evening Prayer:

____

____

____

Take Time to Ask

"Continue to ask, and God will give to you. Continue to search, and you will find. Continue to knock, and the door will open for you. Yes, whoever continues to ask will receive. Whoever continues to look will find. And whoever continues to knock will have the door opened for them."

Matthew 7:7

These verses are a powerful statement about the nature of God and the power of prayer. They reveal a God who is eager and willing to give, a God who desires to be found, and a God who opens doors for those who persevere. They hold immense relevance for us today. We are called to live lives of prayer, to actively seek God's will, and to persevere in our faith. Whether we are facing personal struggles, seeking direction, or simply wanting to deepen our relationship with God, these verses remind us that He is available, willing, and eager to respond. It assures us that God is a God of generosity who desires a relationship with us. It challenges us to be proactive in our faith, to seek God, to knock on His door, and to persevere in our pursuit of Him. By embracing these principles, we can unlock a deeper spiritual life and experience the fullness of God's love and grace.

Heart Work

Intentional Breaths: Close your eyes. Now take a deep breath and slowly exhale. Repeat 4 times. When you're done, come back to this page and imagine that there are no obstacles in your way what would you ask God for? Write out your morning prayer.

Morning Prayer:

What have you been seeking that you have not found? What have you asked for that you have not received?

Mindful Intentions: Find a quiet space Minimize distractions by choosing a quiet and comfortable place. Pick a question, select one that resonates with you in the present moment. Focus on inquiry, not answers. Be patient.

Positive Affirmations: Take this time to write out 1 or 2 positive affirmations that you can repeat to help ask with sincerity and boldness.

Evening Prayer:

Your Plan vs God's Plan

"The heart of man plans his way, but the Lord establishes his steps."

Proverbs 16:9

We make plans, meticulously crafting blueprints for our future, yet life often throws unexpected detours and roadblocks, leaving us questioning the very nature of our existence. We have the ability to plan and shape our futures. From childhood dreams to long-term goals, we create life stories driven by hope, ambition, and a belief in our own power. These plans can be practical or idealistic, blending logic and emotion. However, this desire for control often makes us feel vulnerable when the unexpected happens.

Navigating the tension between our plans and God's plan requires a shift in perspective. Accepting the possibility of a divine plan can offer comfort and purpose, reminding us that even in the face of hardship, there is a larger narrative at play. Conversely, embracing our own will allows us to actively participate in shaping our lives, and making choices within the framework of our beliefs and values.

Ultimately, the key to navigating this internal struggle lies in developing a deep sense of faith and trust. This doesn't necessarily mean blind acceptance but rather a willingness to accept the unknown, to find meaning in the unexpected, and to trust that even when our plans are disrupted, there is a higher purpose at work. It's about cultivating a sense of surrender, accepting that we may not always understand God's plan, but believing that it is ultimately for our good.

It is a journey of constant questioning, seeking understanding, and ultimately, trusting in a power greater than ourselves. By embracing the inherent uncertainty and the possibility of divine guidance, we can discover a profound sense of purpose and meaning, even as we navigate the unpredictable tides of life. The journey itself becomes an act of faith, a testament to the enduring human spirit seeking connection with God.

Heart Work

Intentional Breaths: Close your eyes and release any preconceived ideas of what your life is supposed to be. Now take a deep breath and slowly exhale. Repeat 4 times. When you're done, come back to this page and write out your morning prayer.

Morning Prayer:

____

____

____

____

What was your plan for your life? How has that plan worked out thus far? Do you believe it is time to pivot and embrace a change in plans?

____

____

____

____

Mindful Intentions: Empty your mind of everything you have absorbed from social media and the world that tells you how your life should be or where you should be in life at this moment.

Positive Affirmations: Take this time to write out 1 or 2 positive affirmations that you can repeat to help you let go of any preconceived ideas about how your life should be.

____

____

Evening Prayer:

____

____

____

____

A Prayer for Clarity

Heavenly Father,

You are the source of all knowledge, wisdom, and truth. I come to You today in need of mental clarity. I know that You are able to provide me with the insight I need to move forward in life. I ask that You reveal to me any areas of confusion, uncertainty, and difficulty in my life. Give me a greater understanding in any situations that may be troubling me. I thank You for the gifts You have already given me, and I recognize that You have given me the ability to reason, to think, and to understand. I am very grateful for these gifts, but I am in need of greater clarity.

God, because you are not the author of confusion or chaos, please remove any person, place, or thing that may be clouding my judgment and my mind and preventing me from making clear, decisive decisions. Open my mind and my heart to Your truth. Help me to see things from a new perspective, your perspective. Help me to think more clearly. Grant me the discernment and insight I need to make wise decisions. I pray that You would fill me with the light of Your truth and that I would be able to see things more clearly. Increase my faith and my trust in You as You will provide me with the clarity I need.

In Jesus' name, I pray,

Amen

Dream Big. You Serve a Big God

"Now to him who is able to do far more abundantly than all that we ask or think, according to the power at work within us."

Ephesians 3:20

This scripture stands as a powerful testament to the boundless power of God, a verse that has inspired countless Christians throughout history. It reads: " Now to him who is able to do far more abundantly than all that we ask or think, according to the power at work within us." This passage, nestled within Paul's eloquent explanation of God's grace and the unity of all believers, offers a profound insight into the nature of God's power and its potential in the lives of His children. The verse unveils three key elements: the ability of God, the scope of His power, and the source of that power.

The Ability of God: The opening phrase, "Now to him who is able," establishes the foundation of the verse. It asserts God's infinite capacity – He is not limited by our human understanding or the constraints of this world. His ability is absolute, a promise of limitless possibilities. The Scope of His Power: The verse then clarifies the extent of God's power, emphasizing that He can "do immeasurably more than all we ask or imagine." This statement goes beyond a simple guarantee that God will fulfill our requests. It assures us that He can surpass our wildest dreams and expectations. It speaks to a power that operates outside the boundaries of our limited human perception. We can confidently approach God with our needs and desires, knowing that His power extends far beyond anything we could conceive. The Source of Power: Finally, the verse identifies the source of this boundless power – "according to his power that is at work within us." This vital element shifts the focus from God's power as an external force to the dynamic interplay between His power and our lives. God's power is not merely an abstract concept; it is actively working within us, empowering us to achieve things we never thought possible. This implies a partnership, a collaboration between us and God, where our potential is unleashed through His grace. This verse transcends mere theological understanding and has profound practical implications for our everyday lives. It inspires us to: Embrace bold prayers: knowing God's ability, we can pray with confidence, daring to ask for things beyond our own comprehension. Live with fearless faith: The verse fuels our faith, reminding us that God's power is not static but dynamic, constantly working within us to achieve His purposes. Seek God's will: It encourages us to seek God's will in our lives, recognizing that His power is the driving force behind our successes and the source of our strength.

Trust in the Unknown: The verse reminds us that God's plans are often beyond our understanding, and in His power, we can trust the unfolding of His purposes.

Heart Work

Intentional Breaths: Close your eyes and take a deep breath and slowly exhale. Repeat 4 times. When you're done, come back to this page and write out your morning prayer.

Morning Prayer:

Ephesians 3:20 stands as a beacon of hope and a call to action. How are you going to use this knowledge to seek God's will, pray with confidence, and live with fearless faith?

Mindful Intentions: Write out your dream in detail. Include steps that you need to take in order to turn your dream into a reality. Prayer over your dream to make sure it aligns with God's plan for your life.

Positive Affirmations: Take this time to write out 1 or 2 positive affirmations that you can repeat to help you recognize the power that works within you.

Evening Prayer:

Decision Making 101

Embarking on a spiritual or life journey can be an exhilarating and transformative experience. However, it can also present numerous challenges and decisions that require careful consideration. To navigate these decisions wisely and set yourself up for a meaningful and fulfilling journey, it is essential to approach decision-making with a clear understanding of the principles involved.

1. **Introspection and Self-Reflection.**

The first step in making informed decisions on your spiritual journey is to engage in deep introspection and self-reflection. Take time to explore your motivations, values, and beliefs. Ask yourself why you are embarking on this journey and what you hope to achieve. Understanding your own desires and aspirations will provide a solid foundation for decision-making.

2. **Seek Guidance and Support.**

While introspection is crucial, it is also valuable to seek guidance and support from others who have walked similar paths. Consider connecting with mentors, spiritual advisors, or like-minded individuals. Their insights and experiences can offer valuable perspectives and help you make informed choices.

3. **The Principle of Non-Attachment.**

One of the fundamental principles of spirituality is non-attachment. This means not clinging to specific outcomes or expectations. Instead, approach decisions with an open mind and willingness to let go of preconceived notions. This will allow you to embrace new possibilities and experiences.

4. **Trust Your Intuition.**

In addition to logical reasoning, intuition can be a powerful guide in spiritual decision-making. Pay attention to your gut feelings, hunches, and inner voice. Trusting your intuition can lead you towards choices that align with your higher self and spiritual growth.

5. **The Importance of Patience.**

Spiritual growth is a journey that unfolds over time. Avoid rushing into decisions or making choices out of desperation. Be patient with yourself and allow the process to unfold naturally. Trust that the universe will guide you towards the right decisions when you are ready.

6. **Accept Imperfection.**

There will be times when you make mistakes or feel lost on your spiritual journey. This is a natural part of the process. Instead of beating yourself up, accept your imperfections and learn from your experiences.

7. **Seek Inner Peace.**

Ultimately, the most important decision you can make on your spiritual journey is the one that brings you inner peace. When you make choices that resonate with your values and align with your purpose, you will find a sense of tranquility and fulfillment.

Heart Work

Intentional Breaths: Close your eyes and take a deep breath and slowly exhale. Repeat 4 times. When you're done, come back to this page and reflect on the 7 principles on the previous page. Write out your prayer morning prayer.

Morning Prayer:

Which of the 7 principles do you feel will be the most challenging to implement on your journey? Why?

Mindful Intentions: Be clear about what you want. Start by getting very clear about what you desire in your life. State your intentions often. Practice patience and persistence. Align actions with intentions. Reflect and adjust as needed.

Positive Affirmations: Take this time to write out 1 or 2 positive affirmations that you can repeat to help you recognize the power that works within you.

Evening Prayer:

A Prayer for Guidance

Dear God,

I look to no one else for wisdom. I humbly ask for Your help in making one of the most important decisions in my life because I don't know how to make it without You. Please, give me direction and wisdom so I can make the right decision and bring glory to Your name. I come to You because I ask You for the patience to keep myself from making rash decisions. Give me calmness and composure for every decision in my life, big or small. God, grant me patience even if the road seems long, and stop me from rushing my choices.

Lord, so many choices are laid out in front of me. Please grant me the Holy Spirit's direction and guidance to resolve this problem. It is through You that I know where to go, so I humbly request Your wisdom. I pray to You for protection from temptation and evil that may sway me from making the right decision. Reveal to me the righteous path and help me make a choice that You will approve.

Abba Father, I have been asked to make a major decision, but I don't know how to choose. My mind is clouded by uncertainty, and only You can remove this fog. Lord, I ask You to rid my heart of hesitation so that I can make the choice that glorifies You without any doubt. Please guide me through Your plan and give me the conviction to stay on Your path through whatever challenges may arise. I pray for Your constant presence and wisdom as I walk on this journey.

Lord, draw me closer and closer to You, through Christ Jesus, and reveal to me, in me and through me those treasures of wisdom and knowledge, that I may walk in wisdom and not stumble in the decision(s) I face. Grant me the wisdom to see which decisions of mine will bring calm in my life and the lives of others. Let my life—and especially the choices I make reflect Your wisdom and bring about the blessing of which Your Word speaks.

In Jesus' name, I pray,

Amen

Prioritize Moment by Moment

"For everything there is a season and a time for every matter under heaven."

Ecclesiastes 3:1

This verse, often quoted in various contexts, encapsulates a fundamental truth about life: it is a variety of experiences, each occurring at its designated time. It is not about resisting change or clinging to the past. Instead, it encourages us to embrace the present moment, knowing that every season, and every experience, has a purpose. This acceptance fosters a sense of peace and allows us to approach life with a sense of understanding and gratitude.

While the verse doesn't explicitly mention God, it can be interpreted as hinting at a divine order and plan. It suggests that there is a higher purpose behind the timing of events, even if we may not always understand it. This can bring comfort in moments of hardship, reminding us that even in the darkest times, there is a reason, a purpose, for what we are experiencing.

The beauty of Ecclesiastes 3:1 lies in its assertion that every season is valuable, regardless of its inherent nature. It reminds us that even in times of suffering or disappointment, there is something to be learned, something to be gained. By recognizing the purpose and meaning within each season, we can find greater fulfillment and wisdom throughout our lives.

The verse encourages us to embrace the full spectrum of life, embracing both the joys and the sorrows, the successes and failures, the good times and the bad. It is in the complex mosaic tiles of our experiences that we find meaning, growth, and ultimately, a richer understanding of ourselves and the world around us.

Heart Work

Intentional Breaths: Close your eyes and take a deep breath and slowly exhale. Repeat 4 times. When you're done, come back to this page and identify areas of your life that need to be reprioritized. Write out your prayer morning prayer.

Morning Prayer:

____

____

____

____

Prioritize the areas/situations/people etc., that you identified during your intentional breathing exercise. Focus on the top 5.

____

____

____

____

Mindful Intentions: Based on your new priority list, you may need to create new "boundaries". You may have to have "hard discussions". Be prepared by recognizing and honoring the emotional and conversational boundaries of both you and the other person. Understand that No, is a full statement that does not require further explanation.

Positive Affirmations: Take this time to write out 1 or 2 positive affirmations on how you will honor your journey and your boundaries.

____

____

Evening Prayer:

____

____

____

Defeating Discouragement

Discouragement is a common experience that can affect our motivation, productivity, and overall well-being. It occurs when we encounter obstacles, setbacks, or negative experiences that make us feel defeated or hopeless. While discouragement is normal, prolonged or severe discouragement can have detrimental effects on our lives.

The first step towards defeating discouragement is to identify its source. By understanding what triggers our feelings of inadequacy or despair, we can develop targeted strategies to address them. Common sources of discouragement include: failure or setbacks, negative self-talk, comparison to others, loss or disappointment, and stress. Discouraging thoughts often stem from negative self-talk. When we experience setbacks, it's easy to focus on our shortcomings or the negative aspects of the situation. To combat these negative thoughts, we need to challenge them and replace them with more positive and realistic ones. Reframe the situation: Instead of dwelling on failure, focus on the lessons learned and the growth opportunities. Identify positive aspects: Even amid challenges, there are often positive aspects or silver linings that we can acknowledge and appreciate. Practice positive self-talk: Remind yourself of your strengths, accomplishments, and the qualities that make you valuable.

Dwelling on the past or worrying about the future can magnify feelings of discouragement. Instead, focus on the present moment and what you can control. By taking small, manageable steps toward your goals, you can build momentum and gradually overcome discouragement.

Defeating discouragement is not always easy, but it is possible. By identifying the source of our discouragement, challenging negative thoughts, focusing on the present and future, seeking support and encouragement, and practicing self-care, we can cultivate a more resilient mindset and overcome the setbacks that life throws our way. Remember, discouragement is temporary, and with determination and a positive outlook, we can prevail.

Heart Work

Intentional Breaths: Close your eyes and take a deep breath and slowly exhale. Repeat 4 times. When you're done, come back to this page and identify areas of your life where you self-criticize. Write out your prayer morning prayer.

Morning Prayer:

____

____

____

____

____

Take a moment to reflect on how you see yourself. Write what you see.

____

____

____

____

____

Mindful Intentions: Practice Self-Care. Taking care of your physical and mental health is essential for defeating discouragement. Engage in activities that bring you joy, reduce stress, and promote overall well-being. Seek support and encouragement.

Positive Affirmations: Take this time to write out 1 or 2 positive affirmations to calm the criticism.

____

____

Evening Prayer:

____

____

____

____

A Prayer for Defeating Discouragement

Heavenly Father,

In moments of despair and uncertainty, I come before You with a heavy heart. I surrender my doubts and fears, recognizing their hold on my spirit. Please grant me the strength to rise above the discouragement that seeks to cloud my vision and dampen my resolve.

Help me to remember that I am Your creation, endowed with purpose and potential. Let Your light shine upon the shadows in my mind, illuminating paths I may not yet see. Infuse my spirit with courage, reminding me that setbacks are not the end, but rather steppingstones toward growth.

Surround me with love and support, both from You and the community I cherish. May I find solace in Your promises and wisdom in Your Word. Teach me patience as I navigate through frustration and disappointment, and guide my steps as I seek to fulfill my purpose.

Lord, when I feel weary, remind me to rest in You. When I falter, lift me up with Your grace. Let me find hope in the journey, trusting that each challenge shapes me into the person You intend for me to be. Thank You for your unwavering presence in my life. I place my trust in You, knowing that with faith, discouragement can be transformed into strength.

In Jesus' name, I pray,

Amen

SESSION 2

A Measure of Faith

Having a measure of faith encourages personal reflection on one's spiritual journey. Individuals are prompted to assess their relationship with faith and consider how they are stewarding the measure they have received. Are they cultivating it through prayer, study, and community involvement? Understanding that faith may be both a small ember or a raging fire invites believers to be intentional about nurturing their faith, irrespective of its perceived size.

As you work through the pages of this section:

Reflect on how you are cultivating your measure of faith now and how you will begin to cultivate the measure of faith you will receive while on this journey.

During the Dark Days

"Turn back and say to Hezekiah, the leader of my people, thus says the Lord, the God of David your father: I have heard your prayer; I have seen your tears. Behold, I will heal you. On the third day, you shall go up to the house of the Lord."

2 Kings 20:5

Life is a journey filled with peaks and valleys, marked by moments of joy and sorrow, success and failure. The "dark days" of life refer to those times when one feels engulfed by negativity, despair, or hopelessness. These experiences are universally human but can be intensely personal and isolating. Understanding how to navigate through these dark periods is crucial for emotional resilience and overall well-being.

The "dark days" can manifest in various forms: mental health challenges such as depression or anxiety, significant life changes such as loss, illness, or relationship breakdowns, or even periods of existential uncertainty. These experiences can lead individuals to feel trapped in a cycle of negative thoughts, loss of motivation, and a sense of disconnect from those around them. However, within these shadows lies an opportunity for faith and deep trust in God.

The story of Job is a poignant example. Job, a man of great wealth and righteousness, faced immense suffering through the loss of his children, health, and possessions. Despite his overwhelming grief, Job famously proclaimed, "Though He slay me, yet will I trust in Him" (Job 13:15, NKJV). This resolve to trust amidst suffering serves as a model for believers, illustrating that faith is often forged in the fires of adversity.

Prayer can be a lifeline during dark days. It provides an avenue for individuals to express their fears, doubts, and pain to God. Through prayer, one can shift their focus from despair to divine presence, seeking comfort and wisdom that surpasses human understanding. Trusting God also involves moments of silence and listening in prayer. Amidst the chaos of dark days, finding stillness to hear God's voice can be a profound experience.

Understanding that God hears our prayers invites believers to cultivate a deeper prayer life, offering solace and hope in times of despair. It encourages a relationship characterized by authenticity and trust, reminding us that we are never abandoned, even in our most challenging times. As we reflect on this passage, may we find strength in the knowledge that our prayers, no matter how desperate or simple, are met with divine compassion, mercy, and, ultimately, healing.

Heart Work

Intentional Breaths: Close your eyes, take a deep breath, and slowly exhale. Repeat 4 times. When you're done, come back to this page and identify situations that may be causing you to have dark days. Write out your prayer morning prayer.

Morning Prayer:

Identify and name your emotions to help gain a clearer understanding of what you're experiencing.

Mindful Intentions: Allow yourself to feel whatever emotions arise without judgment. Recognize that it's okay to feel sad, angry, or frustrated. Take slow, deep breaths to help calm your mind and body. Recognize moments that bring light and joy into your life.

Positive Affirmations: Take this time to write out 1 or 2 positive mindful affirmations to bring to a place of peace.

Evening Prayer:

Conquering Everyday Frustrations

Life is filled with challenges, both significant and trivial. Everyday frustrations—those minor irritations we encounter on a daily basis—can accumulate and significantly affect our overall well-being. From traffic jams to misplaced keys, these frustrations often lead to a cascade of negative emotions, particularly stress and anxiety. Understanding how to confront and conquer these frustrations is essential for fostering a healthier mental state and improving our quality of life.

Everyday frustrations can stem from a variety of sources. Environmental elements, such as noisy workplaces, overcrowded public spaces, or inefficient public transportation systems, are common irritants that disrupt our peace of mind. The unpredictability of these external conditions can often lead to feelings of helplessness. Miscommunication or misunderstandings in personal and professional relationships frequently result in frustration. Poor communication can lead to conflicts, unmet expectations, and feelings of isolation, further exacerbating daily tensions.

Individuals often set lofty expectations for themselves, leading to frustration when they fail to meet these self-imposed standards. This phenomenon, known as "perfectionism," can create an ongoing cycle of disappointment that hampers personal growth. In our fast-paced society, time is both a valued commodity and a source of frustration. The pressure to meet deadlines or juggle multiple responsibilities can lead to a sensation of being overwhelmed, resulting in increased irritability.

Heart Work

Intentional Breaths: Close your eyes, take a deep breath and slowly exhale. Repeat 4 times. When you're done, come back to this page and reflect on the source(s) that are causing your frustrations. Write out your prayer morning prayer.

Morning Prayer:

After reflecting on the source(s) that are causing your frustrations, what can you do to eliminate them?

Mindful Intentions: Remember that all emotions are fleeting, including frustration. Improve your emotional intelligence. Emotional Intelligence is your capacity to notice and evaluate emotions in yourself and others, and your ability to regulate the way you express your feelings.

Positive Affirmations: Take this time to write out 1 or 2 positive affirmations to get rid of frustration.

Evening Prayer:

A Prayer for Overcoming Frustration

Dear Heavenly Father,

I come before you today with a humble heart, burdened with the weight of frustration. I acknowledge the feelings that consume me, the obstacles that seem insurmountable, and the doubts that cloud my mind.

Help me to find peace in the chaos of my thoughts. Let your wisdom guide me as I navigate my emotions, reminding me that it is okay to feel overwhelmed, yet I am not alone in this struggle. Grant me clarity, dear Spirit, to see the path before me. Let me recognize the lessons hidden within my frustrations, the opportunities for growth and understanding. Teach me to embrace patience in times of challenge and to cultivate resilience in the face of adversity.

Wrap me in your love, that I might release my tightly grasped expectations. Help me to surrender the need for control and to trust in the unfolding of life. May I find comfort in the present moment, accepting what is, rather than lamenting what could have been. Surround me with compassion, so that I may extend kindness to myself and to others. Give me the strength to communicate my feelings honestly and to seek support when needed.

Inspire me to transform my frustration into motivation. Help me to harness my feelings and direct my energy toward constructive action. May I act with determination, guided by a sense of purpose that aligns with my values.

Finally, remind me of the beauty of hope. Help me to envision a future beyond this moment of discomfort, filled with possibilities and new beginnings. Fill my heart with peace and my mind with clarity, as I walk this path toward healing.

In Jesus' name, I pray,

Amen

Be Gentle with Yourself

"Forgive yourself for not knowing what you didn't know before you learned it."

– Maya Angelou

The journey of personal development and self-discovery is a lifelong pursuit marked by constant learning, growth, and adaptation. Maya Angelou, a celebrated poet, author, and civil rights activist, profoundly encapsulated this journey with her quote: "Forgive yourself for not knowing what you didn't know before you learned it." This statement resonates deeply in a world that often pressures individuals to possess instant knowledge and expertise. Its essence lies in the acknowledgment of human fallibility and the necessity of grace in our learning process. From the moment of birth, human beings are in a constant state of evolution. The acquisition of knowledge is driven by curiosity, a fundamental trait that distinguishes humanity. We learn through experience, observation, and reflection. However, the process of learning is often nonlinear and riddled with mistakes, misconceptions, and gaps in understanding. Acknowledging this inherent part of the learning journey is crucial. Ignorance is not a deficiency; rather, it is a natural state of being when one has yet to encounter specific information or experiences. The assertion that one should forgive oneself for past ignorance acknowledges that every individual exists within a unique context influenced by their upbringing, education, culture, and life experiences. It is essential to recognize that not knowing is a fundamental part of the human condition.

In contemporary society, there is often a stigma associated with ignorance. The fear of judgment can lead individuals to harbor guilt and shame for what they did not know or understood poorly in the past. This emotional burden can stifle personal growth and prevent individuals from pursuing new knowledge or experiences. When individuals forgive themselves for their previous ignorance, they open the door to exploration and curiosity. This shift in perspective enables a more resilient approach to learning, where mistakes are seen as integral components of the educational journey rather than as indicators of inadequacy. The acknowledgment of what we do not know creates fertile ground for growth. By embracing ignorance, individuals are more likely to seek out knowledge and engage in lifelong learning. This active pursuit of understanding is vital in an ever-evolving world filled with new information and shifting paradigms. Learning often occurs in the most unexpected moments. By relinquishing the need to be perfect or to know everything upfront, individuals can embrace experiences that challenge their preconceptions and expand their understanding. This transformative learning process often leads to personal insights and breakthroughs that would be impossible under the constraints of self-judgment.

Heart Work

Intentional Breaths: Close your eyes, take a deep breath, and slowly exhale. Repeat 4 times. When you're done, come back to this page and focus on your inner voice, is it harsh or kind and loving? Write out your prayer morning prayer.

Morning Prayer:

Write yourself a letter of forgiveness.

Mindful Intentions: Set aside 10 minutes of uninterrupted time. Think of a peaceful place. Immerse yourself in the energy of the serene environment and enjoy the sense of peace you feel in the moment.

Positive Affirmations: Take this time to write out 1 or 2 positive affirmations to show yourself some love and compassion.

Evening Prayer:

Every Day is a Fresh Opportunity

"The steadfast love of the Lord never ceases; [a] his mercies never come to an end; they are new every morning; great is your faithfulness."

Lamentations 3:22-23

Great Is Thy Faithfulness / Thomas O. Chisholm, 1923

Great is Thy faithfulness, O God my Father;

There is no shadow of turning with Thee;

Thou changest not, Thy compassions, they fail not;

As Thou hast been Thou forever wilt be.

Refrain:

Great is Thy faithfulness!

Great is Thy faithfulness!

Morning by morning new mercies I see:

All I have needed Thy hand hath provided—

Great is Thy faithfulness, Lord, unto me!

These verses from Lamentations 3:22-23 encapsulate a life philosophy that emphasizes renewal, hope, and divine love. In recognizing that every day is a fresh opportunity, we engage with our lives more deliberately and appreciatively. It fosters a spirit of joy and possibility, enabling us to let go of yesterday's burdens and step bravely into the future. Therefore, as we reflect on each morning's dawning light, may we embrace the steadfast love of the Lord, cherish the new mercies, and celebrate the faithfulness that sustains us through all life's seasons.

Heart Work

Intentional Breaths: Close your eyes, take a deep breath and slowly exhale. Repeat 4 times. When you're done, come back to this page and reflect on something that you tried to do on your own accord, and it failed. Write out your prayer morning prayer.

Morning Prayer:

____

____

____

____

What meaningful steps toward becoming the best versions of yourselves and leading a life filled with purpose and passion can you take today?

____

____

____

____

Mindful Intentions: Life transforms when we actively engage with each new day, igniting the potential for change, growth, and fulfillment. Reflect on the opportunities that have been presented today.

Positive Affirmations: Take this time to write out 1 or 2 positive affirmations/actions you will take to acknowledge new opportunities.

____

____

Evening Prayer:

____

____

____

____

____

New Beginnings

"Remember not the former things, nor consider the things of old. Behold, I am doing a new thing; now it springs forth, do you not perceive it? I will make a way in the wilderness and rivers in the desert."

Isaiah 43:18-19

New beginnings are not merely transitions; they are opportunities for reinvention, empowerment, and a deeper understanding of self. The concept of "new beginnings" is often misinterpreted as simply a reset or starting point after failure or loss. However, this perspective can undermine the value of past experiences and the growth that comes from them. Instead, viewing new beginnings as opportunities to begin again—integrating past experiences into future endeavors—allows individuals to embrace change while carrying forward the wisdom gained from earlier chapters of their lives.

Heart Work

Intentional Breaths: Close your eyes, take a deep breath and slowly exhale. Repeat 4 times. When you're done, come back to this page. Write out your prayer morning prayer.

Morning Prayer:

What do you want to begin again from your new perspective of a "new beginning"?

Mindful Intentions: After careful thought and reflection. Create an "opportunity" board. Much like a vision board but you put opportunities that you want to begin.

Positive Affirmations: Take this time to write out 1 or 2 positive affirmations that will keep you focused on new beginnings or opportunities

Evening Prayer:

A Prayer to Release the Past and Begin Again

Dear Heavenly Father,

I come before you today asking that you help me to release the past. The negative experiences, regrets, guilt, and pain from past events or relationships. The weight of these emotions is weighing me down and hindering my ability to move forward. As I acknowledge the past, I am not denying its existence, but rather I am acknowledging its impact on my life. Help me to forgive as you have forgiven not only others but myself, Lord, help me forgive myself for the mistakes and the choices that I made that caused regret, guilt, and shame.

Lord, I am choosing this day, to release the hold these emotions have on me. I am aware that I need your help and that is why I am coming to you. I am grateful for the lessons and growth that have come from my past experiences, even though the parts of my past may have been painful. I want to fully experience life, the present moment and have a better future. I want peace and clarity. I want to be able to focus on your desires and goals for my future.

In Jesus' name, I pray,

Amen

Mid-Course Corrections

Mid-course corrections refer to intentional adjustments in one's path as a response to new insights or shifting circumstances. They can arise from external factors (e.g., changes in career, relationships, or health) or internal realizations (e.g., new values, interests, or passions). These corrections are vital for maintaining alignment with one's evolving identity and can take many forms, such as changing career paths, pursuing new interests, or reevaluating personal relationships.

By embracing adaptability and recognizing the necessity for change, individuals can realign their lives with their authentic selves. The ability to pivot intentionally encourages resilience in the face of challenges and fosters ongoing self-awareness. Ultimately, self-discovery is not a destination but a continuous voyage of exploration, reflection, and transformation, where mid-journey corrections enrich the experience and enhance personal authenticity.

Heart Work

Intentional Breaths: Close your eyes, take a deep breath and slowly exhale. Repeat 4 times. When you're done, come back to this page and pause. Reflect on something you are doing right now. Write out your prayer morning prayer.

Morning Prayer:

Is there something that you are currently doing, and you feel like you're going nowhere fast? Write down what it is and why you feel like it's going nowhere fast.

Mindful Intentions: Notice the stories you are telling yourself. Are they true? Are they realistic? You hold the pen and paper rewrite those stories and make the positive.

Positive Affirmations: Take this time to write out 1 or 2 positive affirmations/actions you will take to guide you through mid-course corrections.

Evening Prayer:

A Prayer for Mid-Course Corrections

Abba Father,

In this sacred space of reflection, I pause in my journey of self-discovery, seeking guidance and clarity. Grant me the courage to embrace change and the humility to accept my evolving self. Help me recognize the signs that prompt a course correction and allow me to release the fear of what lies ahead. As I stand before the mirror of my soul, may I notice the shadows of doubt that veil my true essence. Illuminate the areas where growth is needed and awaken in me a desire for transformation.

Instill in me the strength to let go of what no longer serves me—old beliefs, toxic patterns, and relationships that hinder my progress. May I boldly step into the unknown, trusting that each pivot leads me closer to you and my authentic self. In this moment, I express gratitude for the lessons learned along the way, for the strength gained through struggles, and for the relationships that enrich my experience. Guide my thoughts as I recalibrate my intentions. Help me align my actions with my innermost values, so I may walk the path of integrity, purpose, and love. May this journey be one of continual discovery, renewal, and grace.

In Jesus' name, I pray,

Amen

Be Patient with Yourself

"But do not overlook this one fact, beloved, that with the Lord one day is as a thousand years, and a thousand years as one day."

2 Peter 3:8

Life is filled with unpredictability, and despite our best efforts, outcomes often diverge from our expectations. Whether it's in our personal lives, careers, or relationships, we frequently encounter scenarios where the results do not align with our plans. In these moments of disillusionment, it's crucial to cultivate self-compassion and patience.

Patience, often defined as the ability to wait without frustration, plays a pivotal role in emotional regulation and mental well-being. When we face setbacks or disappointments, our immediate reaction might be frustration or self-blame. These reactions can exacerbate our stress and hinder our ability to navigate the situation effectively. Conversely, practicing patience allows for a more measured and constructive response to adversity.

Adjusting unrealistic expectations is a fundamental step in managing disappointment. By setting more achievable goals, individuals can reduce the frequency and intensity of unmet expectations. This involves recognizing that life is inherently uncertain, and flexibility in our aspirations can lead to greater satisfaction.

Engaging in positive self-talk is crucial during challenging times. Replacing negative affirmations with kind, understanding phrases can facilitate a more patient response. For example, instead of saying, "I can't believe I messed up again," one might say, "It's okay to make mistakes; I'm learning and growing."

When faced with short-term setbacks, it can be beneficial to adopt a long-term perspective. Reflecting on past challenges and how they have contributed to personal growth can provide reassurance. Understanding that growth and development are lifelong processes can foster patience with oneself.

"Be patient with yourself. Self-growth is tender; it's holy ground. There's no greater investment."

– Stephen Covey

Heart Work

Intentional Breaths: Close your eyes, drop your shoulders, and release the tension. Now take a deep breath and slowly exhale. Repeat 4 times. When you're done, come back to this page and write out your morning prayer.

Morning Prayer:

What is something that you believe you should have by now or should have accomplished by now? Who put the time constraint on your goal or vision?

Mindful Intentions: Remind yourself, that you'll get to the "place" when you need to be there. Remove the Rush

Positive Affirmations: Take this time to write out 1 or 2 positive affirmations that you can repeat to help be patient with yourself and your goals.

Evening Prayer:

SESSION 3

Commitment to Growth

Committing to growth means dedicating oneself to continuous personal, professional, and spiritual development. It involves a proactive approach to self-improvement, learning, and adaptation.

Key points/actions for committing to growth:

Always Learning: Keep seeking new knowledge and skills throughout your life.

Self-Reflection: Regularly think about your actions and experiences to understand what you do well and what you can improve.

Open to Change: Be willing to adapt and try new things, even if they are challenging.

Setting Goals: Define clear and achievable goals for personal and professional development.

Resilience: Keep going even when faced with setbacks and view failures as learning opportunities.

Seeking Feedback: Ask for and value feedback from others to help improve yourself.

Mindfulness: Stay present and aware of your thoughts and emotions to make intentional choices.

Positive Attitude: Maintain a positive outlook and believe in your growth potential.

Building Relationships: Create and nurture supportive relationships with mentors and peers.

Self-Care: Prioritize your physical, mental, and emotional health.

Spiritual Growth: Engage in practices that enhance your spiritual well-being.

Accountability: Hold yourself responsible for your progress and regularly review your goals.

In essence, a commitment to growth means continually striving to be better in all areas of your life.

Your Commitment Determines Your Progress

"Commit your work to the Lord, and your plans will be established."

Proverbs 16:3

This verse teaches us that when we set goals and align our plans with God's will, He helps them succeed. God's promise to support our plans gives us confidence that, with Him, we can achieve anything.

The relationship between commitment and progress is a foundational principle that underscores personal development, education, and professional success.

Commitment can be defined as a psychological state that binds an individual to a course of action or a set of goals. It is often the cornerstone of successful personal habits, educational pursuits, and professional endeavors. Without genuine commitment, aspirations remain intangible and unfulfilled.

In a world that frequently rewards instant results, understanding and valuing commitment can help reframe our perspectives on growth and achievement, ultimately leading to fulfillment and lasting success. As we reflect on our individual journeys, we are reminded that the depth of our commitment—in spite of the speed of our progress—shapes our trajectories and defines our accomplishments.

Heart Work

Intentional Breaths: Close your eyes, drop your shoulders, and release the tension. Now take a deep breath and slowly exhale. Repeat 4 times. When you're done, come back to this page and write out your morning prayer.

Morning Prayer:

___

___

___

___

What is something that you started but stopped because it was not progressing at the speed that you thought it should? What is hindering you from making the commitment?

___

___

___

___

Mindful Intentions: Commit to accomplishing a small goal that will help you reach a larger goal.

Positive Affirmations: Take this time to write out 1 or 2 positive affirmations that you can repeat to help you refocus and recommit.

___

___

Evening Prayer:

___

___

___

___

___

Faith vs Fear

"Fear not, for I am with you; be not dismayed, for I am your God; I will strengthen you, I will help you, I will uphold you with my righteous right hand."

Isaiah 41:10

Life's uncertainties can cause deep fear and anxiety. However, in these moments of doubt, faith can be a powerful source of strength and hope. Faith helps us understand our experiences and offers comfort through community support, prayer, and service. By holding onto our beliefs, we are better prepared to handle life's challenges, finding strength in our faith during uncertain times. As we face an unpredictable world, nurturing our faith is crucial for overcoming fears and finding peace and purpose.

Isaiah 41:10 offers a timeless message of hope and assurance. It teaches us about fear, God's presence, our identity in Him, and the strength He provides. This verse reminds us that God is always there to help us. Isaiah encourages us to have faith during uncertain times, showing us the powerful comfort that comes from God's promises.

Heart Work

Intentional Breaths: Close your eyes, drop your shoulders, and release the tension. Now take a deep breath and slowly exhale. Repeat 4 times. When you're done, come back to this page, and reflect on a fear that has kept you from achieving God's plan and purpose for you. Write out your morning prayer.

Morning Prayer:

____

____

____

____

What are you afraid of concerning your spiritual/ life journey?

____

____

____

____

Mindful Intentions: Think of ways you can turn your fear into motivation to increase your faith.

Positive Affirmations: Take this time to write out 1 or 2 positive affirmations that you can repeat to help overcome the uncertainty of this journey.

____

____

Evening Prayer:

____

____

____

____

____

____

Self-Fulfilling Prophecy

A self-fulfilling prophecy is when your beliefs or expectations cause you to act in a way that makes those beliefs or expectations come true.

How It Works

a. Belief or Expectation: You start with a belief or expectation about something.

b. Action Based on Belief: Because of this belief, you behave in a way that supports it.

c. Outcome Occurs: Your actions contribute to the belief coming true.

When used positively, self-fulfilling prophecies can be powerful tools for growth and success. If you believe that God has good plans for you (Jeremiah 29:11), you'll act in faith, make decisions aligned with that belief, and be more open to opportunities. This positive outlook can lead to experiencing God's blessings and seeing His plans unfold in your life. Believing in your ability to grow spiritually can lead you to read the Bible more, pray regularly, and engage in church activities. These actions will naturally lead to spiritual growth, confirming your belief.

When used negatively, self-fulfilling prophecies can be harmful and limiting. If you constantly doubt God's love and care for you, you might distance yourself from prayer and worship, and ultimately miss out on experiencing His presence and blessings. This can make you feel even more distant from God, reinforcing your initial doubt. Believing that you can't overcome a particular sin, or challenge can cause you to give up trying. This lack of effort makes it easier to fall into sin, thus confirming your belief that you can't overcome it.

In the Bible, faith plays a crucial role in the lives of believers. Jesus often emphasized the importance of belief. For instance, in Matthew 9:21, we meet a woman who says to herself, "If I only touch his garment, I will be made well." She had the belief and expectation; she acted on the belief by touching his garment and she received the outcome of the belief.

Heart Work

Intentional Breaths: Close your eyes, drop your shoulders, and release the tension. Now take a deep breath and slowly exhale. Repeat 4 times. When you're done, come back to this page. Write out your morning prayer.

Morning Prayer:

____

____

____

____

Belief or Expectation: Write out your belief or expectation.

____

____

Action Based on Belief: What action are you going to take based on your belief?

____

____

Mindful Intentions: Let the thought of how life will be once you see the outcome or self-fulfilling prophecy occur.

Positive Affirmations: Take this time to write out 1 or 2 positive affirmations that you can repeat to help overcome the uncertainty of this journey.

____

____

Evening Prayer:

____

____

____

____

____

Do It Now

"Don't put it off. Do it now. Don't rest until you do."

Proverbs 6:4

Proverbs 6:4, serves as a compelling reminder of the vitality of action in all aspects of life. By heeding the call to "Do it now" and recognizing the dangers of procrastination, individuals can unlock doors to opportunities and growth that otherwise may remain closed. The imperatives found in this verse resonate with wisdom that transcends time, urging a life lived with intention, purpose, and immediacy. By embracing this directive, individuals can foster a lifestyle that not only benefits themselves but also contributes to the greater good. Are you ready? Ready to do the heart work? Ready to confront or face those things that have been holding you back?

Let's start with prayer.

A Prayer to Step Out on Faith and Trust God

Heavenly Father,

In this sacred moment, I come before you with a heart full of questions and a spirit yearning for courage. Lord, you know the uncertainties that have clouded my mind and the fears that have paralyzed my steps. I acknowledge that trusting you is not always easy, yet I long to dive deeper into your promise that you are with me in every challenge I face.

Help me to remember the countless stories of faith that fill your Word—how you guided Abraham, empowered Moses, and strengthened Peter. Open my eyes to see that walking in faith requires movement, often into the unknown. I ask for the strength to take that first step, knowing that your hand will guide me, even when the path ahead is unclear.

Lord, I surrender my anxieties and hesitations to you. Replace my fears with your peace which surpasses all understanding. Fill my heart with the assurance that you are working all things together for my good (Romans 8:28). May I not be driven by sight but by faith, trusting that you have already paved the way before me.

I pray for clarity in discerning your voice and wisdom in the decisions I face. Please grant me the courage to act upon the dreams and visions you have planted in my heart. As I step out, let me do so with confidence, knowing that I am walking hand-in-hand with you.

Thank you, Lord, for being my rock and fortress. Help me to continuously lean on you and to cherish the beautiful journey of faith. I trust that, with each step I take towards the light you provide, I will not only grow closer to you but also inspire others to seek and trust you amidst their own struggles.

In Jesus' name, I pray,

Amen

Your Purpose

"For we speak as messengers approved by God to be entrusted with the Good News. Our purpose is to please God, not people. He alone examines the motives of our hearts."

1 Thessalonians 2:4

1 Thessalonians 2:4, provides a theological framework for understanding purpose as a divine calling. The apostle Paul reminds us that the ultimate goal of our pursuits should be to honor God and contribute positively to humanity. This echoes the sentiment found throughout scripture, wherein believers are called to serve one another and to reflect God's love and purpose in their actions.

The verse suggests that while humans may strive to fulfill their desires, the examination of motives by a higher authority adds a layer of depth and accountability to the quest for purpose. It indicates that purposive living involves a moral compass, guiding actions towards not merely self-serving aims but also the betterment of society.

Purpose can be understood as the driving force that motivates individuals to pursue their goals and aspire to personal growth. It embodies one's values, aspirations, and the impact one wishes to leave on the world.

The journey to find one's purpose often begins with introspection. Engaging in self-reflective practices such as journaling, meditation, and mindfulness can help individuals clarify their values and aspirations. Questions to consider may include: What activities make me feel fulfilled? What values matter most to me? How do I want to impact the world around me?

Finding purpose is not a linear process; it requires openness to change and the willingness to adapt. Life experiences, challenges, and new interests may shift one's understanding of purpose over time. Embracing this fluidity is crucial in sustaining motivation and fulfillment.

Purpose becomes tangible through action. Once individuals have a clearer sense of direction, setting short and long-term goals aligned with their purpose can further solidify their commitment. It is essential to break goals into manageable steps, facilitating progress and sustaining motivation.

A Prayer to Discover and Understand Your Purpose

Dear God,

I come before You with an open heart, seeking clarity and understanding. I am grateful for the gift of life, the experiences that have shaped me, and the lessons learned along the way. I recognize that my journey is unique and woven into the larger tapestry of existence. Help me to look inward and uncover the passions that ignite my spirit and the values that resonate within my soul. Guide me to see the possibilities that lie ahead and to embrace the talents You have bestowed upon me. May I find courage in the face of uncertainty and trust in the path laid out before me.

As I navigate the complexities of life, grant me the wisdom to recognize opportunities for growth and connection. Allow me to let go of fears and doubts that hinder my progress. Help me to understand how I can contribute to the well-being of others while remaining true to myself. In moments of confusion, may I find solace in Your presence, reminding me that I am never alone on this journey. May my heart remain open to the signs and synchronicities that guide me toward fulfillment. Thank you for this opportunity to seek and understand my purpose. I am ready to embrace the journey ahead.

In Jesus' name, I pray,

Amen

Spiritual Growth Chart

Purpose: This Spiritual Growth Chart is designed to help individuals track their progress and set intentional goals as they embark on their spiritual life journey. It provides a structured approach to spiritual development, focusing on key areas such as prayer, meditation, study, community, service, and personal reflection. This Spiritual Growth Chart is a flexible guide to support your journey. Use it as a tool to help you stay focused, inspired, and connected to your spiritual path.

Dedication

Goal:

- Commit to a regular spiritual practice.
- Set a daily prayer or meditation routine.

Study

Goal:

- Deepen understanding of spiritual texts and teachings.
- Read and study sacred texts.

Prayer and Meditation

Goal:

- Deepen prayer and meditation practice.
- Extend the duration of prayer/meditation sessions.
- Explore different types of prayer (e.g., contemplative, intercessory).
- Practice mindfulness throughout the day.

Community and Fellowship

Goal:

- Strengthen connections with a spiritual community.
- Participate actively in community events and services.
- Volunteer within the community.
- Establish a support network of like-minded individuals.

Service to Others

Goal:

- Integrate service into spiritual practice.
- Identify and volunteer for service opportunities.
- Practice acts of kindness and generosity daily.
- Reflect on how service aligns with spiritual values.

Inner Transformation

Goal:

- Experience a deep, inner transformation.
- Engage in regular self-reflection and examination.
- Work on releasing negative patterns and habits.
- Embrace forgiveness and compassion.

Living Spiritually

Goal:

- Live a life fully aligned with spiritual principles.
- Make decisions based on spiritual values.
- Practice gratitude and presence in daily life.
- Strive for balance and harmony in all areas of life.

My Future Goals:

Personal Reflection and Adjustment

Monthly Check-In:

1. Reflect on progress in each area.
2. Adjust goals and activities as needed.
3. Seek feedback from a mentor or spiritual guide.

Yearly Review:

1. Evaluate overall growth and development.
2. Set new intentions for the coming year.
3. Celebrate achievements and milestones.

Notes: Remember, spiritual growth is a personal and ongoing journey. Progress may not always be linear, and that's okay. Be patient with yourself and stay open to the process.

Mindfulness Activities

Gratitude Meditation - When you wake up and before you go to bed list 3 – 4 things you are grateful for. Spend 5 minutes focusing on these things and the joy that they bring to your life.

Body Love – Hug yourself and appreciate each body part or body function for what it was designed to do. Apologize to any body part or function that you may have neglected over time and be intentional about caring for your body.

Cultivate Happiness – Think of a time when you were happy. Sit in that moment in that feeling for as long as you can.

Breathe Easy – Start by taking a deep breath. Hold the breath for about 5 seconds. As you slowly exhale, let go of all thoughts that cause anxiety or concern. Acknowledge the power of your breath.

Meet yourself – Sit or stand in front of a mirror. Smile at yourself. Ask yourself how you would perceive yourself if you met yourself in public. Notice and acknowledge your positive qualities (maybe you have nice eyes or a beautiful smile).

Open Your Heart – Relax your mind and body. As you take a breath, imagine that as you do, your heart opens up like a flower. As you exhale, place your hand on your chest and feel the rhythm of your heartbeat. As you feel your heartbeat and connect with the rhythm notice how it makes you feel.

Laugh – Laughter triggers the release of endorphins, the body's natural feel-good chemical. Find something that makes you laugh (a comedy show, cat videos on the internet, etc.)

Block Out Distractions– Create a space in your home that is clutter-free. Put your phone on do not disturb and turn on sounds that calm you and you can focus on your breathing, prayer, and meditation.

Mindful Shower or Bath – Using aroma-therapy candles or bath gels, create an atmosphere where you can wash away the day and reset mentally.

Affirmations/ I Am Statements

Use these pages to write down and keep track of your affirmations

1.____________________

2.____________________

3.____________________

4.____________________

5.____________________

6.____________________

7.____________________

8.____________________

9.____________________

10.____________________

11.____________________

12.____________________

13.____________________

14.____________________

15.____________________

16.____

17.____

18.____

19.____

20.____

21.____

22.____

23.____

24.____

25.____

26.____

27.____

28.____

29.____

30.____

"I AM who I AM Becoming."-Jocelyn Jones

Prayer for More of God

Dear God,

I have tasted Your goodness, and it has both satisfied me and caused me to thirst for more. I am aware of my need for more grace. There are things that my heart is afraid to give up and let go of and I do not attempt to hide these things from You. I come trembling bringing them to You.

Please root from my heart all these things which I have cherished and placed above You, so that You may enter and dwell without rival. I repent for being preoccupied with visible things. Heavenly Father, fill me with longing. Show me Your glory. Say to my soul "Rise Up" then give me grace and strength to follow r lead and the boldness to show the world.

In Jesus' name, I pray,

Amen

Prayer for Rest

Dear Heavenly Father,

As I experience overwhelming seasons of stress and restlessness; help me to remember Your word and promise, "I am with you and for you. I am your peace, and I will give you rest." Father, I am emotionally exhausted and mentally spent from relational challenges. Keep me from giving up on hope and giving in to foolish ways of dealing with my pain and longings.

Father, the stress about health issues, financial pressures, old heart wounds with lingering effects or new heartaches, fears about world crises, and worries about today's unknowns, give me mercy and grace tailored for each situation that might cause my faith to decrease and doubt to increase. Lord, make it undeniably clear to me, that You love me, and that You are in control.

God, at this moment I feel the weight of the world on my shoulders. Things in my life feel like more than I can handle on my own. I come to You as my place of refuge and lay all of my cares at Your feet. I thank You that Your word reminds me to come to You when I am feeling weary and that You promise to bring rest to my soul. Help me to walk in Your rest... to be able to see the goodness of the Lord in the land of the living. Remind me of all the ways You have been faithful to me in the past so I can look forward with confidence, knowing You will take care of me! I declare that I will trust You with every detail of my life and I will give all of my cares to You. Your word says that You know every hair on my head. You care about all things in my life. I do not have to be afraid! You are my safe place. Allow me to find the strength I need to move forward in You.

Father, I thank You that Your Word reminds me that You have given me the power to be brave and to control my thoughts. I ask that in this moment where my thoughts feel like they are out of control, give me a sound mind. Allow me to capture every thought that would want to cause me to have a spirit of fear. Remind me to think about what is good, true, noble, right, lovely, and admirable. Empower me to cast down any thought that would cause me stress, anxiety, or fear. I thank You for all the good gifts You have given me in my life.

Help me to remember them rather than fixate on the things that trouble my mind. I thank You that I can trust in You with all my heart because You promise to lead me on Your straight path. Direct each of my steps. Grant me wisdom so I can move forward with peace.

Strengthen my weary mind, body, and spirit. Help me to run and not grow weary, to walk and not grow faint. I thank You, God, for being my ever-present help, anytime I face troubles. I can't make it without You. Thank You for carrying my load so I can continue to do the good You have called me to.

Reveal to me both the beauty in the work and the rest. Calm my anxious thoughts and encourage my heart with Your nearness. Instruct me in Your ways. Bring productivity and contentment out of the peace and comfort I find. Settle me in Your truth and Your love.

Help me to set healthy boundaries and prioritize by Your Holy Spirit. I have my to-do list, but what do You have for me today? Help me not to miss Your divine appointments. Set my focus on things above and keep my eyes on You. Reveal to me what I should hold on to, and what I need to let go. Empower and equip me for the work You have for me. Give me the lasting strength of abiding in You. Renew my mind, body, and spirit.

Help me to accept Your invitation to come empty and receive the rest I need. Help me to willingly release my fear, my worries, my agenda, and my to-do list. Ease the tension and replenish my body. Silence the voices of doubt and speak Your words of truth. Remove the heaviness of my day and pour out abundantly into my life. Fill me with Your peace, joy, and love. Fill me until the overwhelm is consumed by Your grace, and my life reflects the beauty of resting in You.

In Jesus' name, I pray,

Amen

Prayer for Strength

Dear Lord,

Thank you for all You have given me and for all that You have done for me. You have given me life and You have blessed me with many wonderful gifts. I thank You for the love, joy, and peace You have given me and for the strength You have provided for me throughout my life.

Lord, today I ask that You give me even more strength. I need inner strength to face my current challenges. I need the courage to take the necessary steps to overcome them. I need the perseverance to stay the course and not give up. I need the trust to believe that You will provide me with the strength I need.

Lord, I reach out to You for Your guidance. Please show me which way to turn. Calm my anxious thoughts, speak to my mind. Strengthen me as I falter and feel weary. Allow me to feel strength rising up within my heart. Bring clarity into my visions and dreams. I trust that You are with me, no matter where I go, or what I decide to do. I know that You are always with me and that You will never leave me. I know that You will never give me more than I can handle. I have faith that You will give me the strength to handle any situation and overcome all obstacles.

I thank You for the many blessings You have given me and for being a constant source of strength. I thank You for the guidance and the wisdom You have provided throughout my life. Please continue to guide me and provide me with the strength I need to overcome the challenges I face.

In Jesus' name,

Amen

Prayer to Release Guilt and Shame

Dear Heavenly Father,

I come before You today with a heavy heart and a deep sense of guilt and shame. I come knowing that I need to repent but I want to do it from a humble and sincere heart and Lord in this moment, I am not in that place. This guilt and shame have consumed me, making it difficult to move forward. They have caused me to become angry and have led to feelings of anxiety, and sadness. They have caused me to want to seek revenge. They are currently an obstacle to happiness and peace.

God, please help me to find the courage and strength to forgive myself. Help me to let go of the guilt and shame that I am carrying and replace it with Your love and mercy. Help me to remember that vengeance is Yours. Help me to move on and to live a life of joy and peace. I ask all of these things in Your holy name.

In Jesus' name, I pray,

Amen

Prayer to Release Anger

Dear Lord,

I come to You in a time of need, asking for Your help in releasing the anger I feel inside. I understand that anger is not sin, yet I also know that it can lead to sin and cause hurt to those around me. I understand that it is not wrong to get angry, but I also understand that I must be careful not to let it consume me. I know that anger can be a powerful emotion and that I should not react or overreact while angry.

Lord, is this anger going to be used to reveal my passion and purpose? Will it be used to push me closer to You? Help me to recognize the things that cause me to get angry. Lord when I am feeling anger, help me to express it in a healthy way. Grant me the wisdom to understand what is causing me to be angry and to address it in a way that honors You and benefits others. Help me to use my anger to bring about positive change, instead of allowing it to lead me down a path of destruction.

Give me the strength to release my anger to You and to replace it with peace and understanding. Fill me with Your love and grace so that I can be a source of comfort and strength to those around me. Help me to be a light in this world and to bring Your love and truth to others.

In Jesus' name,

Amen

Prayer of Obedience

Lord, I come before Your throne of grace asking that You would give me wisdom & discernment. I ask that You heal everything in me that keeps me from moving forward in You. My heart desires to walk faithfully in obedience to who and what You have called me to be and do in You. I pray that Your perfect will and Your way be done in my life. Father, help me to take every thought captive. Help me surrender my heart and life to You in true obedience and godly humility. Help me draw closer to You as You do a good work in my life. Build me up, where Christ is the cornerstone. Help me to realize when the Holy Spirit is prompting me, guiding me, encouraging me, and training me.

I surrender all I am to You today and pray that I may walk in newness of love and humble obedience all the days of my life. I want to live godly in Christ Jesus. I ask that You help me to develop an attitude of obedience to Your will and an increasing trust in Your Word. Help me to grow in grace, to develop the right godly practice and purpose in life, so that You are lifted up in my heart and glorified in all I do. As I praise You without ceasing, help me to develop an attitude of prayerfulness – and help me to be obedient to carry out all that I am called to do as a child of God – so that You increase as I decrease. Lord, the eyes of my heart are on You and my confidence is in Your Word. Inspire, convict, teach, and correct me.

I pray that I will develop a teachable and correctable spirit, in submission to the leading and guidance of Your Holy Spirit. Help me to look into the mirror of Your Word and let its truth search out areas in me that need to be rooted out. May I grow in humble obedience to Your ways and help me to reflect the love of the Lord Jesus in my walk and word. Lord, lead me on the righteous path that You would have me go and help me not to rely on my human knowledge and strength, but help me to depend implicitly on Your godly wisdom and power, knowing that we do not fight against flesh and blood but against principalities and spiritual powers in high places.

Give me the spiritual wisdom to step out in faithful obedience on those occasions when I am called to say or do something that is outside of my comfort zone and to follow in the path of those like Queen Esther, who was called for such a time as this. Keep my heart open to Your promptings help to me grow in my faith, and obedience to Your praise and glory. I want to learn to be obedient and to be responsive to Your voice.

Lord, although I do not pray for sufferings in my life, I do ask that like my Savior, I may learn obedience – even if it means that like Jesus, I too have to go through suffering. Give me ears that are open to Your voice. Give me eyes that are ready to see the spiritual lessons that You desire to teach me. Give me a heart that is receptive to Your Word of truth. Give me the grace to pray, "Your will not mine be done". I commit to You my desire to acquire a lifelong habit of spiritual response.

In Jesus' name, I pray,

Amen.

Prayer for Favor

Dear Heavenly Father,

Thank You for always having my best interest at heart. Thank You because every good and perfect gift comes from You. Lord, thank You for helping me realize that I can only work, but a favor that brings real blessings only comes from You. You promised me in Your word, that if I commit whatever I do into Your hands, that You will bless me and cause the works of my hands to prosper. So, I ask that You release Your favor upon my life – a favor that will cause me to excel in every area of my life. Anoint me with Your oil of gladness so that my blessings will flow effortlessly. I ask for Your divine favor and supply of all my needs according to Your riches in glory. Increase my faith, so that Your blessings will not take me out of faith. Lord, thank You for being always mindful of me. Thank You for bringing me this far, and for Your favor that accompanies me wherever I go and in everything that I do. Let Your mercy, grace, and favor manifest in all aspects of my life. Cause favor finding expressions in my life today and always.

Father, thank You for being attentive to my prayers. Your presence brings protection, favor, and peace. I pray that You bless me to experience favor from You and with men. Cause me to receive preferential treatment everywhere I go and prosper me in everything that I do. Raise people in higher positions who will use their power and influence to help me in ways that I cannot help myself. Father, thank You for making me righteous and accepted through the Blood of Jesus. Because of that, I am blessed and highly favored by You. I am the object of Your affection. Your favor surrounds me as a shield, and the first thing that people come into contact with is my favor shield. Thank You that I have favor with You and man today. I pray that Your favor goes ahead of me today and every day of my life. Father, I thank You that You have prepared a table before in the presence of my enemies. Abba Father, grant me the great expectations that I have for this day and for every day of my life. God, thank You for being the miracle-working God and for being my provider. Your word tells me that if I ask, it will be given, if I seek, I shall find, and if I knock, the door shall be opened. Therefore, I ask that You listen to my supplication and grant me favor that will provoke an unusual breakthrough in my life. Make my life an epitome of blessings, so that men will see, and it causes men to draw closer to You and You alone will get all of the glory.

Your power is limitless, and Your strength has no end. Father, all my life You have been faithful. I ask for Your supernatural favor in my life, and I trust You completely to grant me this heartfelt request. Your word reminds me that even if my faith is as small as a mustard seed, it can still cause You to move mountains on my behalf. Lord, I know that You are able to do far more than I can ask, think, or imagine, according to Your power that works in me. Thank You, for being the same yesterday, today, and forever more. Lord, everything that You have Your hands on is transformed in a powerful way, cause Your power to transform my life for good. Release Your favor upon me that will transform my circumstances and rearrange everything around me. I know that Your thoughts and plans for me are thoughts and plans to prosper me and not to harm me, plans to give me hope and a future.

Thank You for all of Your blessings that are perfect. Thank You for being faithful to me, despite my shortcomings. Help me to trust in Your ability to favor me and to bring a turnaround in my situation. My vows to You will be fulfilled because You will answer my prayers. I will remain confident in Your ability to favor me because Your word assures me that those who see You lack no good thing. Lord, as I seek You for direction, guidance, and favor in my life, cause Your hand of favor to rest powerfully on me so that I will see Your victory in all aspects of my life. May nothing stand against my favor and prosperity. Favor me, keep me, prosper me, and cause Your face to shine upon henceforth and forever more. My praise awaits You, Father. Amen, Amen, and Amen.

In Jesus' name, I pray,

Amen

Prayer While Grieving

Lord,

I am in distress; my eyes grow weak with sorrow, my soul and body with grief. My heart is broken, my mind exhausted. I cry out to You and hardly know what to ask. All I can do is tell You how I feel and ask You to keep track of all my sorrows and collect all my tears, as I pour them out to You.

Jesus, You said, "Blessed are those who mourn, for they will be comforted". I am mourning and pleading that You send me Your comfort now. Wrap Your arms around me and hold me tight. Send angels of mercy to me. Shower Your comfort on me through those around me and keep far from me those whose words and actions are no comfort.

Lord, please take the consuming anguish I feel right now. Heal my broken heart and bind up my wounds. I need Your peace. I need "the peace of God, which surpasses all understanding" to guard my heart and mind. I need peaceful sleep. I ask for peaceful thoughts and emotions to rule my days and nights as I navigate through life in this time of grief.

Lord, draw close to me and rescue me. Help me not to grieve like those who haven't discovered Your kindness and mercy, who have no hope; lift me up and give me hope. Help me to believe that tomorrow will be better, and the next day will be easier. Help me to believe that a day will come when I will feel a surge of energy and expectation for what You are doing and where You will take me.

In Jesus' name, I pray,

Amen

Prayer of Protection

Almighty and Merciful God,

I humbly come before You in need of Your protection. I seek shelter in Your loving arms, knowing that You are my refuge and strength. I know that You are the ultimate deliverer, the one who can guard me against all forms of danger and harm. I ask for Your protection from temptation and sin. Help me to stay pure and holy before You, resist the devil's temptations, and abide by Your laws. Guide me on the path of righteousness and keep me from all evil.

Lord, I also seek protection from physical harm and danger. Shield me from enemies, accidents, and illnesses. Be my guardian and protector and keep me safe from all harm. I pray for Your protection in my home, and for my family. Watch over us as we go about our daily lives and bless us with Your peace and presence. Protect us, Lord, from the spiritual darkness that is all around us. Fill us with Your light and joy and show us the way to true freedom and peace. Surround us with Your divine hedge of protection. Lord, I ask that You protect our minds and strengthen us in the power of Your might. Protect us from all evil and keep our souls. Guard our going out and our coming in.

Lord, I pray for emotional, physical, and spiritual protection. Guard my mind against negative thoughts. As I interact with others, let me be a beacon of Your love and peace, reflecting Your goodness in all that I do. I put my loved ones into Your hands, knowing that Your watchful eyes are upon them. Shield me from the worries of the day and the anxieties that try to invade my sacred time of rest. Guard my mind, Lord, from troubling thoughts, and grant me the peace that surpasses all understanding. Let Your holy angels stand guard, keeping the night's darkness at bay and ensuring the safety of me and my family.

Lord, dismantle the attack of the enemy and let Your Spirit whisper words of comfort and reassurance to my soul. Protect my dreams, allowing only what is pure and true to dwell in my heart, my mind, and in my soul. Charge Your angels to stand guard at our doors, keeping away distress and negativity.

In Jesus' name, I pray,

Amen

Prayer for Healing

Loving and All-Powerful God,

I come to You now seeking comfort and strength in a time of need. I ask for Your healing touch to be upon us. I seek Your healing grace for our injured bodies and weary souls, both for myself and for those whom I love. I know that You are the Great Physician and that You are willing and able to heal us. I believe that You can and will do more than I can imagine. I trust that You will heal us so that we can be free from pain and hurt and that You will restore us to full strength.

God, I place my faith in You. I place our healing in Your capable hands. I know that You have the power to heal us and make us whole again. Lord, I also know and acknowledge that you have given doctors the knowledge and ability to assist you in our healing process. I ask that You guide these earthly physicians' hands with Your hands as they work on our bodies. Keep them in their right minds and be with them in every decision that is made concerning us.

I thank You, Lord, for Your healing grace. I ask that You bring us complete healing and restoration. I pray for Your healing power to be released in our bodies and for all pain and suffering to be eliminated. I pray for physical healing, for those who suffer from injury, illness, and disease. I pray for emotional and mental healing, for those who struggle with depression and anxiety. I pray for spiritual healing, for those who have lost hope, peace, and joy.

Lord, I thank You for Your love and care. I thank You for hearing our prayers and for bringing healing into our lives. I thank You for the healing power that You have given us. I thank You for Your grace and mercy. I thank You for always being with us in our times of need. Lord, restore us and make us whole. Fill us with Your presence, Your peace, and Your joy. Bless us with Your love and grace.

In Your holy name,

Amen

Prayer for Clarity

Heavenly Father,

You are the source of all knowledge, wisdom, and truth. I come to You today in need of mental clarity. I know that You are able to provide me with the insight I need to move forward in life. I ask that You reveal to me any areas of confusion, uncertainty, and difficulty in my life. Give me a greater understanding in any situations that may be troubling me. I thank You for the gifts You have already given me, and I recognize that You have given me the ability to reason, to think, and to understand. I am very grateful for these gifts, but I am in need of greater clarity.

God, because You are not the author of confusion or chaos, please remove any person, place, or thing that may be clouding my judgment and my mind and preventing me from making clear, decisive decisions. Open my mind and my heart to Your truth. Help me to see things from a new perspective, Your perspective. Help me to think more clearly. Grant me the discernment and insight I need to make wise decisions. I pray that You would fill me with the light of Your truth and that I would be able to see things more clearly. Increase my faith and my trust in You as You will provide me with the clarity I need.

In Jesus' name, I pray,

Amen

Meet the Author
Jocelyn Jones

Jocelyn Jones, a South Carolina native, is deeply committed to the transformative journey of healing and personal growth. Through years of inner work, she has mastered the art of setting and maintaining healthy boundaries and nurturing relationships. In her debut book, Jocelyn offers the practical tools and insights that have guided her, inspiring others to begin their own journey toward healing, self-discovery, and empowerment. In her current profession, Jocelyn is currently a Human Resource professional working in the learning and development sector. She holds a bachelor's degree from Strayer University in Criminal Justice and has certifications in diversity, equity and inclusion, and change management. She is also currently pursuing her master's degree in professional development from Amberton University. Jocelyn enjoys gardening, meditating, and spending time with family. She is married with two children and Nana to two grandchildren, Rylei and Titan. Jocelyn's journey is also marked by her continued faith in seeking a deeper connection with God, which provides the foundation for her work and life. Her faith guides her daily and fuels her commitment to helping others unlock their fullest potential. Jocelyn's life and work embody her commitment to growth, connection, and her faith-driven mission to inspire others on their own transformative journeys.

All Scripture quotations, unless otherwise indicated, are taken from the King James Version OR ESV Versions of the Holy Bible.

Printed in the United States of America

ISBN: 979-8-89660-628-4

Published By: On the Write Track

Made in the USA
Middletown, DE
03 February 2025

70775566R00044